they fly... or jump... or creep or crawl

D1317267

Contents

ZZZZZZZZ

Insects eat more plants than all the other creatures on Earth put together.

ZZZZZZZZ

Insects have lived on Earth longer than we have. In fact they were around when the dinosaurs lived on Earth millions of years ago.

One in four animals on Earth is a beetle.

I know what an insect is!

I know insects are small and wriggly, but how do I spot one? Remember, all adult insects have **three** body parts and **six** legs.

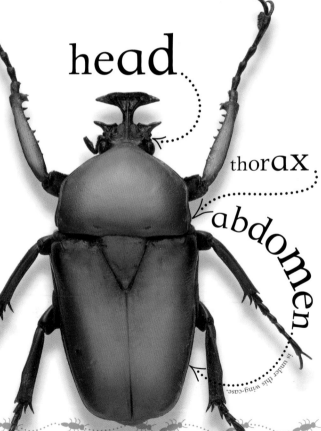

head

thorax

abdomen

leg

is under this wing-case.

4

3 body parts

The body parts are called the **head**, **thorax**, and **abdomen**.

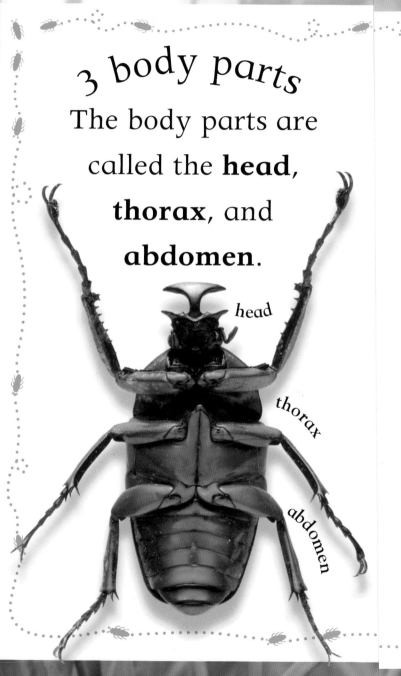

head

thorax

abdomen

Which of these is **not** an insect?

Insects everywhere!

There are over a **million** different types of insects in the world—that's a lot! And they live all over the place—from jungles and deserts to your own garden.

6

Insects c[...]

There c[...]

the people[...]

Moving around

Insects are very good at getting around.
Some **crawl**, others run, a few leap,
but what most do really well is **fly**.

buzzZZZ

flitter

flap

Dragonflies can fly
forward and backward!

flutter

Some insects flap their wings
a thousand times a second.

8

Crawling

Most insects, such as ants and beetles, can crawl along the ground. But flies can crawl up walls and even across ceilings. That's because they have sticky pads under their feet.

Hummingbird hawkmoths hover above flowers.

lacewing

tongue

This moth unfolds its long tongue and sips nectar from inside flowers while it's still flying.

Buzz, buzz, buzz! When insects' wings flap really fast they sometimes buzz.

9

Making more insects

You are never far away from an insect, because insects lay lots and lots of **eggs**. The babies grow inside the eggs until they are ready to hatch out.

Moths and butterflies can lay hundreds of eggs at a time.

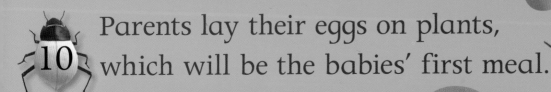

Parents lay their eggs on plants, which will be the babies' first meal.

Curly tongue

A butterfly has a long tongue, called a proboscis, that it uses to suck up flower nectar. This can be so long that the insect curls it into a coil when it is not drinking.

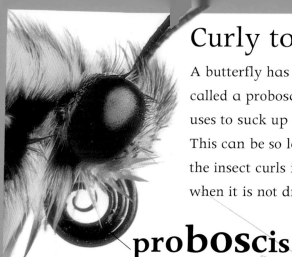

pro**boscis**

crunch, crunch!

This leaf cutter ant has strong jaws that snip through leaves like scissors.

Defense

Insects have enemies. They would make a tasty **meal** for many animals, so they have to find ways to keep safe.

Can you see a **moth**?

Is this an owl's eye?

Quick, hide!

Look carefully. Can you see a green insect? This amazing katydid looks just like a leaf.

A hoverfly looks like a wasp, which stings, so it doesn't get eaten.

eye

I'm a real wasp.

copycats

in disguise

This orchid mantis looks just like a flower.

Can you see the stick insect?

15

Armies and swarms

When locusts swarm together, their dull skin becomes bright and colorful.

The...   ...ne insects that ...enormous ...ng bees, ...es. They ...nd look ...ether.

Locusts swarm together to find food.

A swarm means lots of insects gathered together.

Bees

Honeybees make honeycombs in their nests. Honeycombs have lots of little holes that hold an egg, a baby bee, or a store of honey.

Living with insects

Insects live all around us and are useful for food and clothes—they even help to make more **flowers**.

poll

Bees

Flowers are bright to attract bees to them. Flowers need bees to move pollen from plant to plant.

Beehives

We like to eat honey, which bees make. Some people keep bees in hives. They collect the honey and put it into jars.

19

LONDON, NEW YORK, MUNICH,
MELBOURNE, and DELHI

Written by
Penelope Arlon
Edited by
Penny Smith
Designed by
Sonia Moore and Mary Sandberg

DTP designer: Almudena Díaz
Production: Claire Pearson
Publishing manager: Sue Leonard
Art director: Rachael Foster

First American Edition, 2006
Published in the United States by
DK Publishing, Inc., 375 Hudson Street,
New York, New York 10014

06 07 08 09 10 10 9 8 7 6 5 4 3 2
Copyright © 2006 Dorling Kindersley Ltd.

A Cataloging-in-Publication record for this book is
available from the Library of Congress.

ISBN-10: 0-7566-2226-3
ISBN-13: 978-0-7566-2226-8

Colour reproduction by Media Development and
Printing, United Kingdom
Printed and bound in China by
Hung Hing Printing Co., Ltd

Discover more at
www.dk.com